The Big Cats

A Play

Alec Baron

Samuel French — London
New York — Sydney — Toronto — Hollywood

CHARACTERS

Lily
Joe, her husband
Ann, a social worker

The action of the play takes place in the living room of Lily's house

Scene 1   Night
Scene 2   The morning after
Scene 3   Some weeks later. Day
Scene 4   Christmas Day. Afternoon
Scene 5   Some weeks later. Day
Scene 6   That night
Scene 7   The following morning

Time—the present

THE BIG CATS*

SCENE 1

*The living-room of a two-up, two-down back to back terraced house.
Night*

*The room is furnished with a settee, two armchairs and a coffee table
around the open fireplace. There is a sideboard, a table and two
chairs, and other dressing to suggest the clutter that has accumulated
throughout Lily's married life, for she has lived in this house for all of
this time. The effect is one of cosiness and warmth. Just out of sight
are the front door and scullery*

As the CURTAIN *rises the stage is empty. After a moment Lily enters
from the bedroom. She is a determined, courageous lady who at
times looks to be under fifty, as now, but at others to be a great deal
older. She is wearing a heavy, worn dressing gown*

Lily I'll bet it's cold in that bed, Joe. I was going to put a hot water
bottle in, but it's been so warm lately. Turned nippy now,
though. (*She gets her purse from the sideboard, sits down at the
table and begins to count the money in it*) Sixty . . . sixty-five . . .
sixty-seven . . . one pound sixty-seven . . . one pound sixty-nine
. . . (*She thinks for a moment, sighs, goes to a shelf and picks up a
jug. She empties the contents on the table, sits down and begins to
count again*) What did I say, one pound sixty-nine? . . . And fifty
. . . I'll never get used to this damned new money with all these
big numbers . . . sixty-nine and fifty . . . that's a hundred and
nine . . . that's two pounds and nine pence . . . (*She continues to
count*) . . . two pounds nineteen . . . two pounds twenty-four . . .
two pounds twenty-seven . . . three pounds twenty-seven. (*Calling off, to the bedroom*) It's all right, Joe. We can manage it. (*She

---

*N.B. Paragraph 3 on page ii of this Acting Edition regarding photo-
copying and video-recording should be carefully read.

stacks the money neatly, gets up and replaces the jug) The jug's empty. First time ever! Good job there's enough food in the house until Thursday. (*She places the money on the sideboard*) When he comes, it'll be ready for him. (*She settles herself in an armchair*) Darned nuisance, him always coming on a Wednesday for his money when pension day's Thursday. It would be a lot simpler the other way round. One of these weeks we're not going to have enough if something unexpected comes up. (*She sighs, then, reassuringly*) Don't worry, Joe, I'll see it doesn't happen. Thank the Lord we've never had to ask anyone yet to wait for their money. It's always been there on the nail. On the nail! If he only knew how much we have left. (*She laughs to herself*) Never mind, as far as he's concerned there's plenty more where that came from and there's no-one to tell him different, I won't tell and you won't! (*She gets up, goes to the sideboard to collect the crockery, and starts to lay the table for breakfast with one cup, saucer, plate, knife and spoon*) They say people get large sums of money these days when they give up work. We could have just done with something like that, couldn't we Joe? A few hundred pounds just now would have come in very handy, saved us worrying every time we switch on a light or boil up a kettle, wouldn't it? There's one or two things I'll be needing, too, now the nights are beginning to draw in. (*She sits down, pausing to think*) There's never been a time when there hasn't been a few pounds rolled up in that jug, ever since we got married.

Joe (*off*) Lily . . .!

Lily Yes, I'm coming, Joe. (*She gets up, with a little difficulty*) Hope you've warmed that bed up a bit. You better brace yourself for a shock, my feet are like two lumps of ice!

She switches off the light and exits to the bedroom

SCENE 2

The following morning. The sun is streaming through the window

Joe wanders in from the bedroom, yawning. He looks to be no more than fifty. He is wearing an old cardigan

Lily enters from the scullery, in an old-fashioned pinafore. She has a bowl containing two large potatoes which she begins to peel very carefully

Lily You know that girl that married Mrs Grayson's lad, the one that's moved in with them?
Joe The one with that coloured hair? (*He moves to the window*)
Lily Well, she was saying that people don't peel potatoes any more, they just wash them and eat them, peel and all. She says they've found out the peel's the best part.
Joe Maybe that's why pigs are so healthy.
Lily If the skin is the best part why have folk been peeling them for thousands of years? Some people will believe anything! I mean, you don't eat the skins of bananas, do you, or oranges?

Joe is looking out of the window and not really listening

Joe Nice day again.
Lily Real Indian Summer we're having. I always like a bit of warm weather late on. It's like chipping a bit off the winter.
Joe Yes, but an extra bit of winter gets added on at the other end, to make up. There's nothing for nothing in this world.

Lily stops what she is doing, and muses. Joe continues looking out of the window

Lily Remember that year poor Simon was studying for that last exam he took? Weather was glorious. I hated to see him sitting in that room there all day, working. You kept saying it will change tomorrow, get cold, start raining. Bound to, you said. But it didn't, it just got hotter. Right till the last day of his exam.
Joe Waste of time, all that work he did.
Lily I've never thought that. He got a lot of satisfaction out of passing those exams. So did we.
Joe Yes, but what for? He never made any use of it.
Lily That wasn't his fault.
Joe No. (*Thinking back*) I suppose he might have done if . . .
Lily (*quickly breaking in*) Well he didn't, did he? I think I'll do some washing, there's a few things in the basket. Might as well, while the weather's good enough to hang it out.
Joe Here's the postman. There's a letter for us.
Lily I'll get it! (*As she goes to the door*) It'll be an advert, I expect, that's all we ever get.

Joe Or a bill.
Lily No it won't be a bill, we don't owe anybody.

Lily exits to collect the letter and returns

You're right, it must be a bill. It's from the council. That's all we
ever get from them, bills. (*She reads it, then drops her hand
holding the letter and stares straight ahead*)
Joe What's up?

Lily does not reply

What does it say?
Lily It says they're going to demolish this area—Stanley Street,
Livingstone Place, Victoria Street, Albert Grove, Albert Ter-
race ...
Joe That's our street!
Lily ... the whole neighbourhood!

Joe lets this sink in

Joe What about us?
Lily We're to be moved.
Joe Where to?
Lily (*looking at the letter*) Webber Court.
Joe Where's that?
Lily (*looking again at the letter*) Sadler's Green.
Joe That's miles away! It's the other side of town—two bus rides!
Lily (*staring straight ahead again*) Yes.
Joe Webber Court? I've never heard of it.
Lily It'll be flats, you can bet your life on that. Probably a few
flights up, too.
Joe (*trying to take it in*) Webber Court! It'll be named after that
Councillor, the one who came here asking us to vote for him, do
you remember?
Lily They fancy themselves, those fellers, having Courts named
after them.
Joe He was Chairman of the Housing, he said, didn't he?
Lily (*with contempt*) Huh!!
Joe He *said* they wanted to rehouse the people in the old
properties, I remember.
Lily I didn't like the look of that man the moment I saw him. I
didn't vote for him.

Joe You didn't vote for anybody.
Lily It was raining.
Joe (*after a few moments*) When?
Lily On voting day.
Joe No, I mean when are they going to start demolishing?
Lily It doesn't say. There's a form to fill in.

Joe sits. There is silence for a few moments as they let the news sink in

Joe That's a turn-up for the book and no mistake!

Lily sits. She looks at the letter

What are we going to do, Lily?

Lily doesn't reply, but sits thinking. Suddenly her expression begins to harden. She has made up her mind

Lily (*quietly*) I'm not going!
Joe Not going?
Lily They can't make me.
Joe They can you know. They'll just pull the house down.
Lily Not with me in it, they won't. That would be murder. We've lived in this house ever since we were married, haven't we? Why the devil should we move now? They can pull it down when we've gone, that'll be soon enough.
Joe It's not ours, this house. It belongs to them.
Lily Possession is nine points of the law.
Joe It's no use, Lily, you can't play with those people. They do just as they want to do. They've got the law on their side. They are the law.
Lily (*decisively*) I'm not moving out to Sadler's Green. We don't know anyone in Sadler's Green. And I don't like flats.
Joe You've never lived in one.
Lily No, and I'm too old to start now!
Joe (*looking around*) This is a flat, really, when you come to think of it.
Lily This is a house. Two up, two down.
Joe But we don't use the upstairs any more.
Lily Only because we don't need it any more.
Joe That's what I mean.
Lily It just happens to be more convenient with the bed down-

stairs there in the other room. Saves on heating. Cuts out the stairs.

Joe Makes it . . . sort of . . . like a flat.

Lily (*irritated with him*) Only because we choose to use it that way! But the upstairs is there if we want it. There's a lot of stuff up there, where would we put it, in a flat?

Joe We don't need any of that stuff. I'll bet you don't even remember what's up there! Must have gone rotten by now most of it, anyway.

Lily That's as may be. I'm not going!

Joe looks at her as she sits, determined and adamant

Joe But Lily . . .

Lily No!

Joe is silenced

No more Joe! I don't want to go! (*She pauses*) Do you want to go?

Joe No, I don't, of course I don't, but . . .

Lily Well that's settled then. We're not going! (*She tears up the form, defiantly*)

There is a BLACK-OUT

SCENE 3

Some weeks later. Day

Joe and Lily are sitting at the table. Lily is trying to drink a cup of tea which she is finding difficult because they are both helpless with laughter. Joe has no tea

Joe . . . and it was all tied up with a neat little bow . . . (*He demonstrates tying a bow, effeminately*)

Lily (*spluttering*) Stop it, Joe, I can't drink my tea.

Joe . . . and then you plonked the parcel down on the counter and told him to bloody well keep it!

Lily No, I didn't tell him to keep it. I told him to bloody well stuff it!

Joe That's right, you did. Do you remember how his mouth dropped open? He'd gone to such a lot of trouble! He stood there looking like a spaniel that had just had his dinner taken away.

Lily He should have thought of that before he tried to take us on. Damned cheek! He started with the wrong customer, he did! I mean, I knew the price, I'd been in the day before to ask, hadn't I? It was him told me, himself, but he'd forgotten. He asked for nearly twice as much!

Joe Served him right when you marched out of the shop leaving him holding the parcel, wondering what had hit him.

Lily Do you remember that time in that restaurant in Scarborough when the fish was off?

Joe Remember it? I'll never forget it!

Lily I could smell those pieces of fish before they even reached our table. I thought, I hope that's not for us! I wasn't going to eat bad fish and neither were you, and I told her so.

Joe Yes, and then the waitress fetched the manager and he said there was nothing wrong with it and we'd have to pay for it whether we ate it or not. And you said go on then, I'll pay for it, you eat it, let me see you eat it.

Lily He didn't though, did he? (*Very sure of herself*) No!

Joe It wasn't like in that shop though, we were on our own there, but walking out of that restaurant like that with everybody watching ...

Lily If they wanted to eat fish that had gone off, then it was up to them. *I* wasn't going to and I wasn't going to let you either!

There is a knock at the door. Joe and Lily look at each other for a moment, then Lily goes to the window

There's a car outside. I can't see who it is.

There is another knock at the door

Lily moves towards the front door but does not open it

Who is it?

Ann (*off*) Mrs Mee?

Lily Yes?

Ann (*off*) Could I have a word with you, please?

Lily (*exchanging glances with Joe*) Just a minute.

Lily exits to open the door

*Ann enters. She is dressed like a student although she is probably
about twenty-five. She carries a briefcase. Lily follows her in. She
now seems to have aged considerably. Her voice is more croaky
and she moves with difficulty*

Ann Hello. My name's Ann. Ann Raynor. I'm a social worker,
Mrs Mee, from the Welfare Department.

Lily (*suspiciously*) Oh! Are you another one about the house?

Ann (*sidestepping the question*) May I sit down for a minute. My
feet are killing me. (*Without waiting for an invitation she sits*)

Lily (*immediately spikey*) Your feet? You haven't been walking,
you've been driving in that car! What is it you want?

*Ann senses problems but decides not to notice. Joe remains seated at
the table throughout*

Ann (*getting out a file*) Can I get your name right, Mrs Mee? It's
Mrs Joseph Mee, isn't it?

Lily No, not Joseph. My husband was christened Joe. Just Joe.

Ann (*altering the paper*) Mrs Joe Mee. Now, I have a report here
from the Council . . .

Lily I thought so. Well, don't waste your time, I'm not moving. I
told the man who came from the Council weeks ago . . .

Ann Keep calm Mrs Mee. I'm on your side. I've come to see what
we can work out. You see they're going to start demolishing this
area on Monday.

Lily Not this house they're not!

Ann No, not this house, of course. Not yet. A lot of the houses are
already unoccupied, as you will have noticed, and all sorts of
unauthorized people are starting to move in.

Lily If people have no homes what do you expect them to do?
Sleep in a field?

Ann (*ignoring this*) Rather than go to the expense of bricking up
all the doors and windows as the houses become empty, the
Housing Department has decided to start pulling them down.

Lily Do you work for the Housing Department?

Ann I've told you, I'm a social worker. I'm on the Welfare Team,
attached to Housing, but I'm independent really.

Lily Well I'm independent too. There are lots of people still here.
Any number.

Ann Most of them will be moving within the next couple of weeks.
Lily Have they filled in their forms?
Ann You're the only one that hasn't.
Lily And I don't intend to!
Ann Why don't you want to move, Mrs Mee?
Lily I don't have to give reasons.
Ann If I could understand why, I'd be in a better position to help you. You'll be far more comfortable in Webber Court you know, they're very nice flats. Clean and new, with every convenience. Fitted kitchen, built-in wardrobe, the lot. I've got my car here, I've really come to take you along to see one.
Lily There'd be no point. I'm not going to Webber Court, or to any damned Court!
Ann If you talk like that you might find yourself in the County Court.
Lily We'll see about that!
Ann How old are you, Mrs Mee?
Lily That's none of your business.
Ann How long have you been a widow?

Joe sits quite still, and shows no reaction, although he follows the conversation with interest

Lily (*hesitating*) Long enough.
Ann When did your husband die, Mrs Mee?
Lily (*reluctantly*) Eleven years ago, if you must know.
Ann Did you have any children?
Lily Yes.
Ann How many?
Lily One son.
Ann Where is he?

Lily raises her eyes heavenwards

Upstairs?
Lily There's no-one upstairs.
Ann (*slowly understanding*) Oh, I'm sorry. Brothers and sisters?
Lily I don't know what it's got to do with anything, but yes, one brother and one sister. They were much older than me. They've passed on, too. I was the youngest by ten years, an afterthought, or an accident, I never found out which.
Ann So you are virtually alone in the world.

Lily No, not alone.

Ann Who then? Nieces? Nephews?

Lily Never you mind.

Ann (*changing her approach*) Now, if you're worrying about the difficulties of moving, I can make arrangements for everything to be done for you. I can arrange for someone to come and pack and move everything you want to take with you—although I must tell you there won't be room for much, the one-person-flats are not all that big, but nearly everything is provided. They'll unpack at the other end for you, too, and I'll come and take you there in my car, and give you all the help I can.

Lily That's very kind of you ...

Ann Please call me Ann.

Lily ... but I'm not going.

Ann But why, Mrs Mee?

Lily Don't keep saying why! I've told you, I don't have to give reasons!

Ann Oh dear! (*She is not sure which way to proceed*)

Lily What will happen if I refuse to go?

Ann You can't refuse to go I'm afraid, Mrs Mee. If it becomes necessary, the County Court would issue a Possession Order and a County Court official will serve it on you.

Lily Is it a piece of paper?

Ann Yes.

Lily I'll tear that up too, then.

Joe smiles, as if he loves to see Lily with her hackles up

Ann Then the Council would have no alternative but to obtain a Bailiff's Warrant.

Lily (*upset by the word*) Bailiffs?! Could they—remove me—bodily? Lift me up and carry me out?

Ann No, I don't think they would do that.

Lily (*relieved*) Good! Then this is where I stop!

Ann They would probably send a psychiatrist to see if you were in your right mind.

Lily Rubbish!!

Ann It's not, I'm afraid. If he reported that you were behaving irrationally, and he might very well do that, they could then send an ambulance for you, they'd wrap you up in blankets and carry you out as a hysteric. I saw a case like that once. You wouldn't go to Webber Court then, you'd go to a psycho-geriatric ward.

Lily It's them that's crazy, not me. Tell them that.

Ann It's no use, Mrs Mee. In the end, if there was no other way, they could call the police. Then you'd be escorted out.

Lily I thought the police were there to protect my human rights, not the Council's rights!

Ann Look—I don't believe the police should be used in cases like this, you're not a criminal, Mrs Mee. I'm only telling you what they could do.

Lily Then let them come. Let them send the bloody army! I'll be waiting for them!

Ann They're going to pull this house down. You'll have to go in the end, so why don't we make it as pleasant as possible.

Lily It's no use them sending you to try and frighten me. I'm not afraid of them. I'm staying here. They won't pull the house down with me in it. Just let them try!

Ann (*trying to be patient and unwilling to admit failure*) Mrs Mee ... I'm trying to help you. I've told you, I'm on your side, believe me. But there are some things you just can't fight against, and this is one of them. Can't we look at this problem sensibly?

Lily Now you listen to me, miss. You go back to the Town Hall or wherever it is you come from, and tell them they can pull the whole area down—they can pull the whole city down for all I care, but they're not pulling my house down! It's no good you coming here, all honeyed words, and telling me you're on my side and then trying to persuade me to leave. I won't go. (*Suddenly, unexpectedly, she starts to cry, in spite of herself*) I'm an old woman, trying my best to live decently on an old-age pension. This is my home, it's always been my home. My husband and I were happy here, he'd tell you if he could. We had our share of troubles, but we've got happy memories too. We had a good life here. When I'm gone you can do what the hell you like here but not until. Not until, and I'm still very much alive.

Ann, now convinced that she is not going to get any further, stands and gives Lily a card

Ann I'll leave you this. It's got my address and phone number.

Just get in touch if you want me to help you. It's what I'm paid to do. (*She turns to go, then hesitates*) I don't agree with people being made to do what they don't want to do, but I can see their side too. These old terrace houses *need* replacing, even though it means upsetting some people in the process.

Lily That may be your opinion but it isn't mine. (*She stands up with difficulty*) I'm quite happy here and I'm not moving, and that's final. Tell them that, will you?

Ann Yes, I will.

Lily Good-bye then.

Ann Thank you for seeing me. Don't hesitate to get in touch if there's anything I can do.

Ann exits. Lily follows her to bolt the door, then returns

Lily (*as she returns*) Well!! (*She sits*)

Joe Why didn't you tell her?

Lily Tell her what?

Joe You know—about me.

Lily Tell them about you?! Are you crazy?

Joe They might understand then.

Lily That's all I'm short of! You heard what she said—they'd have a head-shrinker here in one-two-three to say I was mentally disturbed or some such rubbish. They'd never understand. They've never lived alone, they don't know what it's like. You're all I have left, Joe. You're all I ever had. I'm not going to spend what's left of my life without you. The pity of it is I can't share you with anyone or they'll think I'm off my rocker. But you're real enough to me, Joe. You understand, don't you?

Joe Of course, I do, Lily, and I'm grateful to you. Without you I ... I wouldn't exist.

Lily So be it then.

Joe (*after a moment*) You won't win, Lily.

Lily It's got nothing to do with winning. I'm not leaving you!

Joe Couldn't I come with you?

Lily You know very well this is where you exist—here, in every corner of this little house, in every room. This is where we exist, the two of us, where we've always existed. If I went there I'd be on my own. There's nothing of you there. I'm used to us being here, together. I can't imagine you and me in new surroundings, can I, in Webber blooming Court? If they pull this house down they'll smother you and me in the rubble, all our lovely memories in these rooms, bury them once and for all, everything that's happened here. They'd bury you with it. They might as well bury me in rubble then, too. I don't want to go there on my own. (*She starts to cry*) I don't want to, Joe ... (*She breaks down*)

Joe sits looking at her compassionately

There is a BLACK-OUT

SCENE 4

Christmas Day. Afternoon

There is a cloth on the table and one place laid. A glowing fire in the grate and two coloured candles on the table provide a warm, cheerful illumination. A sprig or two of holly decorate the room

Joe is sitting at the table, still wearing the same cardigan

Lily, now younger looking and more buoyant again, enters from the scullery with a tiny Christmas pudding with holly on the top

Lily How's that then, Joe? A Christmas pudding! The whole works!

Joe If you think that impresses me, you're wrong. I never understood what you see in Christmas pudding—I hate the sweet and sickly stuff.

Lily (*sitting at the table*) I know, Joe, but don't worry, there's none for you.

Joe There'd hardly be enough there for two people that liked it, anyway.

Lily I bought the smallest size there was. (*She looks at it for a moment, her spoon poised*) I think I'll have it a bit later though, I'm full. It'll make Christmas last a bit longer. (*She pushes it away*) Not a bad Christmas dinner, was it? A bit of turkey, stuffing, veg—and a Christmas pud to follow. Can't be bad. That bonus is a godsend, I wonder whose blessed idea that was?

Joe I'll make you a bet that was the best Christmas dinner in the whole neighbourhood.

Lily Pretty dangerous bet that, Joe, seeing this is the only house standing in the whole neighbourhood.

Joe I only ever bet on certainties, don't you remember?

Lily I don't care if it is the only house standing, I like being here on our own. I feel like the Lady of the Manor—monarch of all I survey—even though it is only a sea of lousy rubble.

Joe And plenty of free firewood.

Lily (*laughing*) Yes, I forgot about that.

Joe Wouldn't surprise me if the house didn't fall in one of these days, then they wouldn't need to pull it down.

Lily Not likely, it's more like a Cathedral than a house now—standing all on its own, with flying buttresses on both sides. Bet it can be seen for miles. Good for another hundred years yet, this house. We should live so long! (*She starts to laugh, then tears begin to well in her eyes, but she continues, smiling through the tears*) I don't mind not having any neighbours, as long as you're here. I would have hated having Christmas on my own. And we'll manage without their damned electricity, one bill less to pay. They've done me a favour, cutting it off, if they but knew . . .

Joe It's a bit dark at night without the street lights, though.

Lily Who cares! We don't need them, we don't go out at night, do we?

Joe And it's a long way to the shops for you now.

Lily I only need to go once a week, I'll manage. (*She is determined to be cheerful*) Hey, I've got another little treat, too. (*She goes to the sideboard and gets a miniature bottle of cherry brandy and a glass*) Look at this! Cherry brandy. Couldn't resist it. I haven't had a glass of cherry brandy since I can't remember when, and you know I've always liked it. (*She opens the bottle and pours. She takes a sip and a rapturous expression comes on to her face*) Hey, that's good! Warms you all the way down. There are some good things in this life you know, Joe. Simple things.

Joe Like what? Cherry brandy?

Lily Like a cup of hot strong tea first thing on a morning. Ecstacy! Like the smell of hyacinths in the Spring. A tiny baby laughing.

Joe Love on the sofa in the afternoon.

Lily Now then Joe, behave yourself.

Joe What do you mean, behave yourself.

Lily It's not nice to talk about those things, especially at Christmas.

Joe We're married, aren't we? There's nothing shameful about a bit of love between husband and wife ...

Lily In the afternoon? On the sofa?

Joe Where does it say in the Bible about having to make love only at night—you tell me that! Or at any particular time! It says nothing about having to do it only in bed.

Lily It doesn't say anything about doing it on the sofa, either.

Joe A bit of love always seemed sort of ... not special to me, at night, in bed.

Lily You're a pervert!

Joe Then be glad of it. Be thankful. Anywhere but bed was better, wasn't it? Remember that time by the haystack in Devon? More of a surprise. Come on, Lily, own up.

Lily Hey, Joe, remember that time when Simon came in and caught us at it? I didn't know where to look.

Joe Go on—he was only five—he wouldn't have any idea what was going on.

Lily Nevertheless, I felt guilty for a month after that. Couldn't look him straight in the face, even though he was just a child. I blush to think of it, even now.

Joe You had too narrow an upbringing.

Lily You've told me that before.

Joe Well it's true. Your folks looked at a bit of lovemaking as though it were a sinful thing to do. Remember that night before we were married when we were saying goodnight on your doorstep and your father came out and bundled me off as though I was trying to burgle the house or something. We weren't doing anything so terrible.

Lily Well, I don't know. If I remember right you were ...

Joe What?

Lily Anyway they could see from the side of the bay.

Joe They shouldn't have been looking. In any case ...

Lily Mother put him up to that. I copped it too, when I came in.

Joe Makes me wonder how they ever managed to have three kids!

Lily I'll bet they never made love in the afternoon, though.

Joe That's their misfortune. They might have enjoyed it. You did, didn't you?

Lily I'm saying nothing.

Joe You were always ready enough when I suggested it.

Lily I was a dutiful wife.

Joe Come off it! No-one ever forced you to do anything against your will, it wouldn't have been possible.

Lily You always talk about me as if I was some kind of . . . ogre. I'm not, am I Joe?

Joe We turned the tables on Simon, though, didn't we, the day we came home and he was on the sofa with that Wilkinson girl, and she was lying there with . . .

Lily (*stopping him*) Don't go into details, I remember it very well. Why did I get so mad with him?

Joe The way you went on anyone would think they were doing something unnatural. They were just enjoying themselves.

Lily I didn't see it like that. It was my upbringing, my parents, coming out in me. Funny how you think "Now how would my mother and father have reacted to that?" Then without thinking you behave in the same way. I've often thought of that afternoon. Poor Simon. We spoiled his fun, didn't we?

Joe He never got to know the joys of being married.

Lily No.

Joe I'm glad he had a few adventures though—boy and girl together. Especially with that girl he met at camp. She looked to me like hot stuff, that one, you could see it in her eyes. There's nothing like it, you know. Nothing. Is there?

Lily I'm too old to remember.

Joe So why do you keep thinking about it all the time?

Lily I don't keep thinking about it all the time.

Joe And why do you try and fool yourself? It's me you're talking to—me, Joe. You can be open with me. Truthful. It won't go any further, you know. I couldn't tell anybody even if I wanted to, could I?

Lily Yes, well, I do think about it a lot I suppose. What else have I to think about, except the happy times we had together? Sometimes I try to live it all over again, right from the very first time we met—from that first time you kissed me at that party. There are long gaps which I can't remember at all. Great blanks. I remember some things I expect, which you've forgotten, just as I suppose you remember things which I've forgotten all about. Pity we can't exchange those memories.

Joe We wouldn't have been able to exchange those memories even if ... you know. You always found it difficult to discuss intimate things. No, not difficult, you found it impossible, for some reason. You've been a lot more ... unreserved ... lately.

Lily Yes, I've noticed that. Do you know, lots of times I wanted to ask you which were the particular special moments we had together that you remember with most pleasure, what we did that you liked the most, what I did that you liked the most ... but I was never able to.

Joe I would have told you.

Lily I know you would.

Joe Lily ...

Lily What?

Joe If you're not going to have your Christmas pudding till later, how about ... a little love in the afternoon?

Lily Joe! I knew that was coming! You never change!

Joe Well?

Lily To be quite truthful ... I wouldn't mind a lay down for a while ...

Joe Come on then.

Lily (*a twinkle in her eyes*) Just for an hour then.

He takes her hand. She blows out the candles, and the stage is in darkness as they go through to the bedroom

SCENE 5

Some weeks later. Spring sunshine makes the unoccupied room look very pleasant

There is the sound of a car arriving outside. The car door bangs, followed by a knock at the door

Lily enters from the bedroom, once again the old lady. She looks out of the window, snorts with displeasure, and sits down at the table. The knock is repeated, but Lily disregards it

Ann (*off, calling through the letter-box*) Mrs Mee—please let me in. It's Ann. Ann Raynor.

Lily (*calling*) Go away! Do you hear me? Go away!
Ann (*off*) It's important! (*She starts knocking again*)

Lily, with a gesture of impatience, goes to open the door

Ann enters followed by Lily

Lily There's no use your coming here again trying to butter me
up, nothing's changed.

Ann sits down

Ann (*almost ominously*) Sit down, Mrs Mee.

Lily does not sit down

Now, you've seen the letter from the Council ...
Lily (*lying*) I've seen no letter from the Council.
Ann Oh come now, you must have done, it was hand delivered.
Lily Really!
Ann You have no postal address any more, you know. Albert
Terrace no longer exists. And the fellow that delivered it
couldn't have got the wrong house, could he? It's the only one
here.
Lily If you must know, I tore it up. I didn't read it.
Ann Oh! (*She can't decide whether to believe her or not*) Well ...
they're coming tomorrow.
Lily Who are?
Ann To demolish the house.
Lily It'll be over my dead body. They'll find themselves in the
High Court never mind the County Court—for murder.
Ann I don't think so.
Lily We'll see.
Ann Mrs Mee, trust me. I'm appealing to you, and I promise you
won't regret it. Let me take you to see the flat that's been
allocated to you ... We can go right now ...
Lily I'm not going anywhere.

*Lily sits adamantly. Ann looks at her for a moment, sees she is not
going to get anywhere, and gives in*

Ann All right then, just sign this paper to say you will move as
soon as you've found somewhere else, made other arrangements, and the Council will hold fire for a while.

Lily I'm signing nothing!

Ann You're a difficult woman, Mrs Mee.

Lily I don't think so. I'm not harming anyone. I'm not asking anybody to do things they don't want to do. I just want to be left alone, in peace.

Ann It's not possible. Don't you see? The Council has been very patient, they've done everything they can.

Lily Then let them pull the flaming house down! I'll be sitting there, right there in that chair.

Ann But . . . it doesn't make sense!

Lily Is that what that head-shrinker said, the one that came here?

Ann No, he said you were of perfectly sound mind, as it happens. He could find no grounds at all for recommending any action.

Lily Good for him!

Joe enters and sits down

Ann, of course, does not see Joe but Lily smiles

Ann The Council has gone through all the legal processes. You are now in breach of the law, you know. You defied the Bailiff's Warrant.

Lily (*snorting*) Bailiffs!!

Ann If, as you say, you didn't read the letter from the Council, then I have to tell you that at eleven o'clock tomorrow morning a policeman and a policewoman will be here to escort you out of the house, and the house will be demolished.

Lily I'll be waiting for them.

Ann They can't force you to go to Webber Court, so you are at liberty to make other arrangements if you refuse the flat that has been offered to you. I'm sorry, Mrs Mee, but they will carry you out, if necessary, for obstructing the course of the law.

Lily We'll see about that.

Ann What can I do to persuade you to accept defeat?

Lily That's a foolish question and you know it. You don't expect me to tell you how you can make me change my mind? You ought to have more sense!

Ann Do you know, Mrs Mee, I meet a lot of old ladies in my work, but I've never come across one as stubborn as you! Most people are reasonable. In a way, I admire you for it, but I just don't understand you.

Lily Don't try.

Ann I can't for the life of me see what there is here to make you want to stay, when there's a nice new flat waiting for you. There's a list as long as my arm of people who'd be only too happy to get the flat you're being offered.

Lily Then give it to one of them—it'll make the list shorter.

Ann I give up! (*She stands*) Anyway, I've told you, they'll be here in the morning. I've tried my best, haven't I?

Lily I'm not blaming you. Go about your business.

Ann If you change your mind . . .

They stand looking at each other

The lights fade to a BLACK-OUT

SCENE 6

The same night. Lily is sitting in the armchair, by the fire. Joe is sitting at the table

Joe Lily . . .

Lily (*as if to herself*) Yes, Joe?

Joe Can I . . . talk to you . . . ?

Lily I'd rather you didn't.

Joe Are you really going to refuse to move tomorrow?

Lily I can be just as stubborn as they can! They can pull this place down on my head if they've a mind to. (*Despondently*) What does it matter!

Joe It matters a great deal. (*He waits for her to speak*) Lily . . .

Lily Shut up, Joe!

Joe You'll do as you like, I know you will. You always did. You never took any notice of me, did you?

Lily What do you mean? Of course I did!

Joe No you didn't, not when it came to important decisions.

Lily Like when?

Joe Like when I was offered that job down South—you said no, *you* weren't moving! I never got another opportunity like that.

Lily Opportunity! We could have landed up a lot worse!

Joe Or a lot better. The work was easier. I might have ...

Lily Stop guessing! There's no point!

Joe And that time when I wanted to buy that new semi near the moor ...

Lily The mortgage on that place would have been a burden round our necks for years!

Joe We could have managed it if we'd have tried, you know we could. That house would have been ours by now. It was only two thousand, five hundred pounds. Must be worth ten times that by now.

Lily There's no use crying over spilt milk! What are you getting at?

Joe You know what I'm getting at. You know what I'm going to say, don't you?

Lily (*raising her voice*) All right, so I do!

Joe Don't let them carry you out tomorrow, Lily. You'll have to go in the end. Do it with dignity. You've made your point, you've held out longer than anybody. Give in, Lily.

Lily No!

Joe For my sake.

Lily You're a right one, you are! It's over you I'm refusing to go.

Joe I know that, and I understand that, and I know just how you feel. But this time I can see sense more clearly than you can. Don't fight them any more, Lily. It's ... wrong ...

Lily Who the hell do you think you are? My conscience? Leave me alone! Stop interfering! I've enough problems without you!

Joe I'm begging you, Lily—out of my love for you—take my advice for once. Give in ...

Lily No! (*She cries*)

Joe Please ...

Lily No! I won't!

Joe Lily ... please ...

Lily (*through her tears*) No! Leave me be! Leave me be ... ! (*She breaks down completely*)

The lights fade to a BLACK-OUT

SCENE 7

Lily is standing at the table tying a length of sisal round a bulging suitcase to make it secure. She is wearing her hat and coat. Joe stands watching her

Lily There! That's that! (*She lifts it off the table*) By, its heavy!
Joe I wish I could help you with it, Lily.
Lily Well you can't, can you, so stop worrying. I'll get the kitchen stuff.

She exits and returns with a cardboard carton of pots and pans

That's the lot. That's all I'm taking.

The clock on the sideboard chimes the half hour

Oh my God, I nearly forgot the clock. Half past. They'll soon be here. I'll put it in with the pots. (*She does so*)
Joe Mind they don't drop it.
Lily I'll watch it!
Joe That was our first wedding present, that clock, do you remember? Never given us a minute's trouble.
Lily I'm not even going to look upstairs, Joe. I wouldn't know what to do with any of that stuff if I took it.
Joe A whole lifetime—in one suitcase and one cardboard carton!

Lily sighs and sits down. They are silent for a moment or two, then Lily is unable to control her feelings. A tear appears in her eye

Now then, Lily . . .
Lily There's no use, Joe. You were quite right, I can't fight against them any more. I did all I could.
Joe I don't mind, honestly, Lily. Don't worry about *me*. (*He sits, rather forlornly*)
Lily Joe . . . we never really had a chance to say goodbye . . . last time . . . when you had your stroke. It was so sudden So unexpected. You seemed as right as rain, and next minute there you were, lying on the floor . . .
Joe I was trying to get up, but I couldn't . . . I couldn't move my hands, or my legs.
Lily I know. I tried to lift you, but you felt like a sack of bricks. When they got you to the hospital and you were lying there on

your side, with your eyes closed and your mouth open, unable to move . . . and I took hold of your hand and spoke to you . . . you seemed to squeeze my hand, ever so gently, didn't you? That's how I knew you could hear me. I tried to tell you . . . I tried to tell you how much I needed you, how much I've always needed you. You could hear me, couldn't you?

Joe I wanted to answer you, but I . . . I couldn't, Lily. I couldn't get the words out.

There is the grinding sound of a tractor approaching outside

What's that?

Lily goes to the window and looks out

They're here, Joe. They've brought one of those . . . bulldozer things . . . to push our house down.

Joe They call them big cats, those machines. It's short for big caterpillers.

Lily Yes, I know.

Joe Funny—you never liked cats, did you?

Lily They're arrogant, cats. Impudent, contemptuous, they do whatever they want to do and you can't stop them, never mind what you might have done for them.

Joe That's true.

Lily Joe . . . I just want to say . . . to tell you . . . you were a wonderful husband, Joe. We had our rows, I know, I must have been a bad-tempered shrew lots of times, but I didn't mean to hurt you . . . and I knew you'd always be forgiving and understanding. It takes two to upset a marriage, Joe, and you would never be one of them, so I knew I was safe. I just want you to know that I'm grateful for the life we had together . . . even though you weren't one of the world's big earners, it didn't matter . . . you made me very happy . . . and I hope I made you happy at least some of the time . . .

There is a knock at the door

That'll be the police. They're early. Don't worry, Joe, I won't let them touch me. (*Calling*) I'm coming.

Lily goes to unbolt the door

Ann enters, followed by Lily

Ann Oh, good, you've got your coat on. I'm so glad. Oh, and
you've packed your things, great! I hoped you'd see sense.
Now—what has to go?
Lily Everything I want is in that suitcase and that carton. They
can bury the rest.
Ann Right. (*She picks up the suitcase*) I'll take this to the car and
come back for the carton.
Lily No, I can bring that.

Ann exits

*Lily picks up the carton and moves to the door. Joe sits in the centre
of the room. Lily stops at the door with her back to him*

Lily Good-bye Joe.
Joe Good-bye Lily. God bless.

Lily exits, closing the door

*Joe sits motionless. The sound of demolition begins as dust falls on
him from above*

The Lights fade to a BLACK-OUT

FURNITURE AND PROPERTY LIST

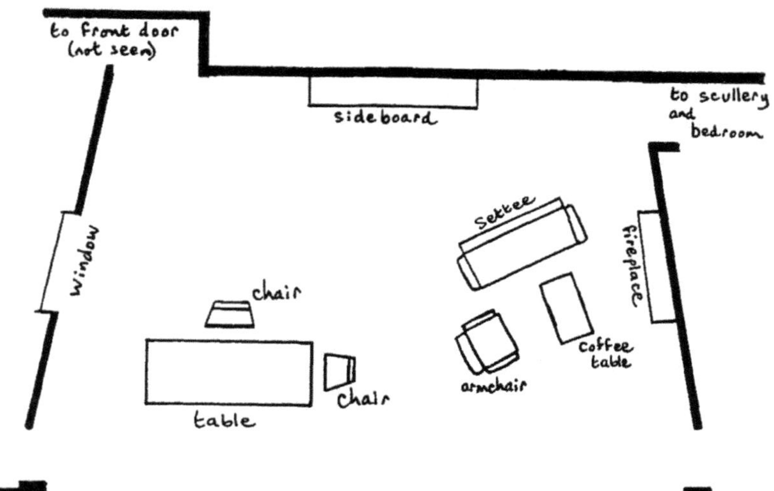

SCENE 1

On stage: Settee
Armchairs
Dining table
Dining chairs
Sideboard. *On it:* chiming clock, purse with money in it. *In it:* breakfast setting for one, miniature Cherry Brandy, glass
Shelf. *On it:* jug containing loose change
Curtains at window (closed)
Coffee table
Dressing as desired

SCENE 2

Strike: Breakfast things

Set: Curtains open

Off stage: Bowl with two large potatoes and knife (**Lily**)
               Letter (**Lily**)

SCENE 3

Strike: Bowl, potatoes and knife

Set: Cup of tea for Lily on table

Personal: **Ann:** Briefcase containing files, papers and business cards

SCENE 4

Strike: Cup and saucer

Set: Cloth on table with one place laid
               Candles (lit) on table
               Sprigs of holly to decorate room
               Fire in grate

Off stage: Small Christmas pudding with holly decoration on top (**Lily**)

SCENE 5

Strike: Table cloth and all Christmas indications

SCENE 6

No props

SCENE 7

Set: Bulging suitcase and length of sisal

Off stage: Cardboard box containing pots and pans (**Lily**)

Personal: **Lily:** hat and coat

LIGHTING PLOT

1 Interior setting. Property fittings required: centre light

SCENE 1

To open: Centre light on

Cue 1   Lily switches off light   (Page 2)
               Black-out

SCENE 2

To open: General effect of bright sunshine

Cue 2   As Lily tears up form   (Page 6)
               Black-out

SCENE 3

To open: Daylight

Cue 3   As Lily breaks down   (Page 13)
               Black-out

SCENE 4

To open: Fire lit, candles alight

Cue 4   Joe blows out candles   (Page 17)
               Black-out

SCENE 5

To open: Daylight

Cue 5   Lily and Ann look at each other   (Page 20)
               Slow fade to black-out

SCENE 6

To open: Centre light on

Cue 6   Lily breaks down   (Page 21)
               Fade to black-out

SCENE 7

To open: Daylight

Cue 7   As dust falls   (Page 2
            Slow fade to black-out

EFFECTS PLOT

Cue 1   **Joe:** "... letter for us."   (Page 3)
            Letter falls through letter box

Cue 2   As Scene 5 begins   (Page 17)
            Car arriving and door banging

Cue 3   **Lily:** "... that's all I'm taking."   (Page 22)
            Clock chimes half-hour

Cue 4   **Joe:** "... get the words out."   (Page 23)
            Tractor approaching

Cue 5   As Lily exits   (Page 24)
            Demolition sounds and dust falls from above

MADE AND PRINTED IN GREAT BRITAIN BY
LATIMER TREND & COMPANY LTD PLYMOUTH

MADE IN ENGLAND

The Birds Stopped Singing

A Play

Lawrence Barker

Samuel French – London
New York – Sydney – Toronto – Hollywood

CHARACTERS

Pavel Alexandrovich, a reporter
Herr Bruno Liszt, a salesman
Erna, a servant woman
Frau Ghirstfeld, a landlady
A Man, salesman
A Woman, prostitute

The action takes place in a room in a roadside inn, several miles from the outskirts of Berlin

Period—mid-January, 1930

PRODUCTION NOTES

Dialogue: no attempt whatever should be made by the actors to acquire or use any foreign accent in their portrayal of the characters.

Lighting: throughout the action of the play the main acting area is the one most strongly lit, the source of light apparently being obtained from the oil or paraffin lamps on the occupied tables, and from the light of the fire. The rest of the room should be much dimmer, and the upstage corners quite dark.

THE BIRDS STOPPED SINGING

A room in a roadside inn. Night, mid-January, 1930

Two doors lead into the room: one from the rest of the inn, the other from the street. Above and below the latter door are windows, the curtains of which are drawn. The room is furnished with six or seven sets of tables and chairs. Three of these sets form the main acting area: one directly opposite the fireplace, one above the fireplace near the wall, and one below the fireplace, also near the wall. The whole appearance of the room is one of drabness, bareness and coldness. The chairs and tables are of assorted sizes, and well worn. The paintwork is dark and dull, the wallpaper yellow and peeling. It is a building that has seen better times, and is now used mainly as a cheap lodging-house by local farm workers and the occasional prostitute looking for trade

When the CURTAIN *rises Pavel Alexandrovich is seated at the table opposite the fireplace, in the chair nearest to the fire. There is another chair at the other side of his table. He is facing slightly front. He is reading a book. On his table there is a lamp, a bottle of Schnapps, a glass and an ashtray. He is forty years old, average build, and he wears a dark grey suit, collar, tie, and black shoes, which are not polished. His general appearance is untidy. He holds his left arm in a stiff, slightly unnatural way. His left hand is covered by a black leather glove. His left arm is in fact false, and when required he is able to position the arm, which is jointed at the elbow and wrist, into as near a natural position as possible, by moving it with his good hand. His face is grave, and set in a way that would indicate to a person who would care to look for such things, that here was a face that has suffered much anguish and pain, and a body, which in the tortuous war against complete alcoholic oblivion, was slowly, ever so slowly, losing the battle. Erna, the servant woman is standing in the middle of the room, her back to the audience. She is laboriously sweeping the floor which is covered with sawdust. She is thirty, average height and build. She wears a simple cotton dress and a large grey apron. Her hair is covered by a plain grey scarf. She is deaf and dumb. The Man is sitting at the*

*table below the fireplace, his back is side on to the audience. He is
twenty-five. He wears a well-cut suit, his collar and tie are undone.
At this moment in time he is very drunk and his complete attention
is taken by his female companion. The Woman, a prostitute, sits
opposite the Man. She is thirty. Her clothes are cheap and obvious
and her make-up is heavy. She is holding the attention of the Man
by sharing the same glass of Schnapps with him, sensually sipping
her own drink, and then teasing the Man with the glass when he
tries to take his. Their heads are very close together, the Man is
completely infatuated*

*The inn is quiet, the only sounds are the brushing of Erna's broom
on the wooden floor, and the low, silly laugh of the Man. Suddenly
there is a banging on the street door. The banging stops, then starts
again after a slight pause. Erna continues with her sweeping and
Pavel Alexandrovich remains perfectly still, reading his book. The
banging continues and increases, and is now very loud. The Woman
turns her head towards the street door, makes a face of annoyance,
and shouts over the noise*

Woman Frau Ghirstfeld. There is someone at the door!

There is no reply; the banging goes on

Frau Ghirstfeld. Someone at the door!

*Frau Ghirstfeld enters through the inner door. She is a rotund
woman of about fifty, with a round kindly face. She is wearing a
simple black dress and an off-white apron. Her head is covered.
Her movements are such as to indicate a person with more than
enough chores to do, and very little time to do them in. As she
enters she is wiping flour from her arms and hands with her apron*

Frau Ghirstfeld Patience! I'm coming. I'm coming. (*She reaches
the outer door and draws the bolt*) Who is it? Who is there? (*She
opens the door*)

*Herr Bruno Liszt steps inside. He also is about fifty, average
height, with a broad, flat face, a heavy chin, and reddish hair. His
clothes are expensive, dark suit, wing collar, black shoes. Under
his top coat he wears a buttonhole. He carries a small black
leather case. As he speaks he removes his hat*

Liszt A thousand pardons for troubling you at this late hour. I
trust you are the landlady?
Frau Ghirstfeld I am.
Liszt Ah! (*A slight bow*) Then may I introduce myself? Herr
Bruno Liszt. Travelling representative. (*He waits for a reaction*)
Frau Ghirstfeld A salesman.

This is not the reaction he expected

Liszt Correct! I realize that it is at very short notice, but may I
enquire as to the possibility of obtaining a room for the
remainder of this—er—disastrous night?
Frau Ghirstfeld Well, Herr Liszt, it is rather late, but if you don't
mind waiting while I finish my baking and prepare you a bed,
then I can make you welcome.
Liszt Excellent. Excellent! (*He crosses to the fireplace and stands
with his back to the fire*) I'm sure you will make me very
comfortable. (*He glances at the Man and Woman, who have by
now resumed their game, and then at Alexandrovich*) Have you
any other guests staying the night?
Frau Ghirstfeld (*moving to him*) I have my regulars, the farm-
workers, but they've all gone up long since. Oh! I hope all
your banging hasn't disturbed any of them. Some are hard
enough to handle at breakfast time as it is. And then there's the
two gentlemen you see here.
Liszt I see. What's happened to the lights?
Frau Ghirstfeld Oh, they went off about nine o'clock, sir. One of
the workers thinks the storm must have brought the lines down
somewhere. Last time it happened we were without for three
days and the wind was so strong it took the slates of the roof.
Thank goodness it's died out now, anyway.
Liszt Well, I find it quite charming. It adds a certain atmosphere.
Don't you agree?
Frau Ghirstfeld Will you be wanting supper, sir?
Liszt Well, if you could manage something it would be welcome.
Frau Ghirstfeld (*thinking*) I could re-heat the broth the men had,
that would help to warm you, but I'm afraid it's just bread and
cold sausage to follow. But if you are really hungry, then I
could . . .
Liszt Please, no. It sounds quite substantial. Perhaps some
brandy while I am waiting.

Frau Ghirstfeld Of course; if your coat is damp, Herr Liszt, I could hang it in your room. It will dry there.

He takes off his top-coat. Frau Ghirstfeld moves to Erna

Erna, leave the sweeping. Come you must help me now.

She signs to Erna to take Herr Liszt's hat and coat and starts to move to the door. Erna nods, stands her broom against a table, then moves to Herr Liszt

Liszt Thank you—(*giving Erna his hat and coat*)—I'll keep my case—(*he taps his case*)—my samples.

Erna tries to reply, but the sounds that come from her lips are only of one syllable

Erna Na . . . Ha . . . Gur.
Frau Ghirstfeld She can't hear you sir, she's deaf. She can't speak either. But she will understand you if you make signs.
Liszt (*smiling at Erna, pointing to his case*) Samples. (*Slowly*) You understand?

Erna shakes her head

S-A-M-P-L-E-S.
Frau Ghirstfeld Best not go on, sir. It will only confuse her. Then she'll get upset, and I'll get no help at all. Come, Erna. (*She signals*)

Frau Ghirstfeld and Erna exit through the inner door

Herr Liszt glances round the room, then at the Man and Woman. By this time they have ceased their game. The Woman is whispering in the Man's ear. Herr Liszt is determined not to have to sit by himself. He moves to Pavel Alexandrovich

Liszt May I join you?
Pavel (*not looking up*) If you wish.
Liszt Thank you. May I introduce myself. Bruno Liszt, travelling representative. (*Pause*) With a name like Liszt I should, of course, be a pianist. (*He sits*) But believe it or not there is a connection. I sell locks you see. Security devices, and locks have keys, so do pianos. Liszt played piano—hence Bruno Liszt (*He laughs slightly; there is still no reaction from Pavel*) It was certainly a stroke of luck finding this place. I was hoping to

drive straight through to Berlin by at least eleven, but I was caught in a fearful storm about an hour back. Probably the same one that passed over here. It certainly slowed me down, I can tell you. Driving was almost impossible. Eventually it eased off, and when I saw this inn, I decided to call it a night and try for a room. (*Looking around the room*) Mind you, it's not what I'm used to! But there it is. Are you travelling into, or out of the city?

Pavel (*looking up for the first time*) I have an appointment in Berlin in the morning.

Liszt Splendid! Perhaps I could offer you a lift.

Pavel I think not, but thank you for the offer.

The Man and Woman rise. The Man is unsteady, the Woman supports him. They exit together by the inner door

Liszt (*indicating their exit with a nod of his head*) Comforts of the house, eh? (*He laughs heartily*) May I ask to whom I have the pleasure of speaking?

Pavel (*after a slight pause, as if not sure whether to tell him or not*) Pavel Alexandrovich.

Liszt (*with surprise*) Russian!

Pavel Yes.

Liszt Ah, my friend, you are a long way from home. A business man, yes?

Pavel Journalist.

Liszt Really, for a German paper?

Pavel Sometimes. I'm freelance.

Liszt Now that I like. A man who is his own master. (*Slight pause*) Your profession must take you to many places.

Erna enters. She carries a tray, on it a half-bottle of brandy and a glass; she serves Herr Liszt

Thank you, my dear. Oh! (*He makes signs*) Thank you!

Erna nods slightly and exits

Yes, many places, and I'm sure you must have some fascinating tales to tell. Hmm . . . (*He pours a drink*) Will you join me? Your glass is empty.

Pavel You are very kind. (*He closes the book and places it on the table*)

Liszt An interesting novel? (*He fills Pavel's glass*)

Pavel It's not a novel. It's a reference book. Civil Engineering.

Liszt Are you an engineer as well as a journalist, or is it merely an interest? (*He drinks*)

Pavel No, I qualified as a Civil Engineer shortly after the war. But I have not ... (*He pauses*) I have not been involved in engineering for some years. I read now only as a form of relaxation.

Liszt You must have a sharp intellect if you can relax that way. I also like to read, but for me it must be a good story, history, adventure, intrigue—love, passion, eh? (*He laughs again*) You mentioned the war.

Pavel drinks

Were you a soldier; did you see active service? I ask because .. Well, forgive me, but your arm, did you lose it fighting—in battle?

Pavel (*with a low, self-mocking laugh*) My arm—no it is not a war wound, but to answer your question, yes, I was a soldier.

Liszt Don't tell me, let me guess. Officer, Infantry. First Russian Army. Correct, yes?

Pavel Almost. Private. Infantry. First Russian Army. I volunteered the day Germany declared war. (*He drinks*)

Liszt Now at last we have something in common. I also was a private, *and* in the Infantry. But it was the German Army of course. (*He tops up Pavel's glass*) I hated it. My first taste of battle was at Tannenburg, absolute slaughter.

Pavel I know, Tannenburg was my first battle too.

Liszt Then we both share terrible memories. (*Pause*) Were you taken prisoner? Many were.

Pavel No. I was not taken. (*He is now deep in thought*)

Liszt You know, my friend, it's a strange world, is it not? Two people, you and I, who were once sworn enemies, and yet here we sit, talking and drinking as though—well, as though it had never happened. Don't you agree?

Pavel What? Oh, yes.

Liszt As I say, I hated it. I lost many good comrades. But through it all, horrible as it was, I had one great regret and that was ...

Erna enters. This time she carries Herr Liszt's supper: a bowl of broth, and a plate of brown bread, and cold German sausage. She places it before Herr Liszt

Ah! Supper. Will you join me, my friend?
Pavel What? Er, no, thank you. I have already eaten.
Liszt Ah, then you will excuse me if I carry on. (*He begins to eat*) Thank you, my dear.

Erna goes to her broom and continues to sweep

As I was saying, horrible as it was, I had one great regret, and that was that in all those four long years whilst I was risking my life, I never once saw the Kaiser, not once! It would have meant so much if on just one occasion the Kaiser had appeared and said "Well done Liszt, you make me proud to be a German," or something like that. (*He stops eating*) Well, it would have made all the difference. It would have helped me to understand the realization of all that I was fighting for. But, he didn't. (*He makes a vague gesture and resumes eating*) This broth is very good! Of course it was different for you Russians. By tradition your leaders marched with you into battle. Tell me, did you ever see the Tsar?
Pavel (*with a slight start*) The Tsar.
Liszt Yes, I know for a fact that he often visited his troops in the front line. Did you ever see him?
Pavel (*turning his head slightly to front*) Yes I saw him, twice.
Liszt Oh, you must tell me about it, please. Somehow it would be like a form of—er—(*he searches for the word*)—er—compensation for me, do you understand?
Pavel I—(*he pauses*)—would rather not. (*He moves to pick up his book*)
Liszt (*stopping him*) Please, it would mean a great deal to me.
Pavel Look, I do know what you are saying, but for me to try to relate those two occasions to you, would only bring back memories that I have spent many years in trying to forget. Besides which, I doubt very much if you will believe me.
Liszt I will. I will. Please. (*He fills Pavel's glass*)

During Pavel's speech, Liszt continues to eat, and Erna quietly sweeps the remaining sawdust into a small pile in the middle of the floor

Pavel (*slowly*) All right—but remember I did warn you. (*He* *drinks)* The first time was about eight months after our defeat at Tannenburg. I had been transferred to another regiment. I had just finished four weeks leave, and the prospect of returning was, as you will recall, not a happy one. I arrived back on the Sunday night, and was soon informed by my fellow warriors, that we were to be moved up to the front the very next day. As usual, it was a rumour that proved to be true. The next day found us, bright and early, marching along a pleasant country road towards the sounds of distant guns. At noon we were given halt, and ordered to fall out. I remember it was a beautiful day, and I just lay on my back staring up at the sky. Somewhere near me a soldier was playing his balalaika, and humming in a low thick tone . . . I was terribly afraid.

Pavel's eyes meet Liszt's. Liszt nods in understanding

I just closed my eyes and wished that it could be an ordinary day. A harvest day back home. Hot and sweaty work, but at the end of it, food and drink, and a good laugh with my mates in the village inn. There was a shout, then another, and a voice cried, "It's the Tsar!" I raised myself upon one elbow, and there he was, the Tsar! He was on horseback and there were three high ranking officers with him, anxiously staring about them. By now everyone was on their feet, and excitedly moving toward him. One of the officers attempted to move his horse in front of the Tsar, to try to protect him, but the Tsar gestured for him to hold. Soon we were all about him, waving and cheering. Then he raised his hand and in an instant there was silence. "My children", he said "I give you my blessing." Then he held up a Holy Icon. As if by a whispered command we all fell down upon one knee, and took off our caps. He lifted the Icon higher and we bowed our heads and joined him in our own private prayer. When we had finished, he slowly moved his horse forward, towards me. The soldiers quietly moving back and making a pathway. He was a few yards away from me when he stopped, and leaned down slightly, out of the saddle. There was a young soldier standing close to him. "Is tomorrow your first battle?" The soldier just nodded. "Are you afraid?" Again the soldier nodded. "So am I." Then he was gone. For a moment nobody moved, we just stood, each of us trying to believe that what we had seen and heard had really, actually happened. Somebody, somewhere gave a loud cheer, and all about me men who had only an hour before cursed the war, and cursed the Tsar, were now laughing and talking, and expressing their doubts that such an impossible happening could have ever been granted to them—and I myself, was not quite so afraid.

Liszt (*quietly moved*) When a man is a witness to such a thing as that, it must remain in his mind forever.

Pavel Yes.

Liszt But I don't understand, why should you want to forget? If it were the other way round, and it had been my experience, I would want to tell about it at every opportunity.

Pavel I said I saw him twice. The first occasion, the one I have just acquainted you with, and the considerable effect it had on me, is very closely linked with my second meeting with him.

Liszt Then please continue. (*He attempts to fill Pavel's glass, but the bottle is empty*) I'll order some more!

Pavel I warn you again, you will not believe me.

Liszt Nonsense. You tell everything so beautifully, why I could almost imagine that I was there.

Frau Ghirstfeld enters from the inner door with a bucket and shovel

Ah! My dear woman, another bottle, if you please! For my friend here.

Frau Ghirstfeld Your room is all ready now, sir. I've put a hot-water bottle in your bed. You should be comfortable. Is your supper adequate?

Liszt Fine, fine!

Frau Ghirstfeld Will you two gentlemen be retiring soon? There is no need to disturb yourselves just yet, but I'm afraid the floor has to be washed. If you prefer it, you could go into the next room. It's quite warm in there, and private.

Liszt No, no. You just carry on. We won't be disturbed. Could I have another bottle please? (*He holds up the empty bottle*)

Frau Ghirstfeld Just a moment if you please, sir. (*She goes to Erna and gives her the bucket and shovel. Then she makes signs*) The hot water is ready now.

Erna nods and begins to shovel the sawdust into the bucket. Frau Ghirstfeld moves to the occupied table

Now sir, what was it you wanted?
Liszt Another bottle. (*He indicates the empty bottle*)
Pavel (*to Frau Ghirstfeld*) Just a minute. Who is going to wash
the floor?
Frau Ghirstfeld Why, sir, Erna of course. (*She looks from one to
the other*) Is anything wrong?

Pavel looks across at Erna and then shakes his head

Pavel No.
Frau Ghirstfeld She'll be very quiet, sir, she won't annoy you.
I'll tell her. (*She goes back to Erna and indicates by holding her
finger to her lips, that Erna must be quiet*)

Erna nods and makes signs that she understands

There sir, she won't bother you now. Brandy is it, sir? (*She goes
to the inner door*)
Liszt (*to Pavel*) Brandy?
Pavel (*after a pause*) Vodka!
Liszt By all means. (*To Frau Ghirstfeld*) Vodka.
Frau Ghirstfeld Right, sir.

Frau Ghirstfeld exits

Liszt Tell me, why did you want to know who was going to wash
the floor?
Pavel Because what I have to say, I can only tell to someone who
I feel would understand. Your reaction to my first story was
the reaction of a man who has seen slaughter and death many
times, indeed, if you had not been moved by what I told you,
then believe me, nothing in this world would make me continue.
To have another person here, to *perform* before an audience,
would be unthinkable. (*He nods towards Erna*) With the woman
it does not matter.

Again their eyes meet

Liszt You make me feel privileged. (*Pause*) Perhaps I am.

*Erna finishes her work and exits by the inner door, taking her
bucket, shovel and broom*

Look—you know I have forgotten your name, please forgive
me.

Pavel It's Alexandrovich, Pavel Alexandrovich.
Liszt Look, Pavel Alexandrovich, if you had rather not tell me, then please, I understand. We can talk about something else.
Pavel No, it is started now. (*Pause*) I *will* finish it.

Frau Ghirstfeld enters with the vodka on a tray

Frau Ghirstfeld Here we are, sir. Will there be anything else? (*To Pavel*) If you like, I can put a water bottle in your bed.
Pavel No. It's all right.
Frau Ghirstfeld Very well, sir. Just shout if you want me.

Frau Ghirstfeld exits by the inner door

Pavel pours the vodka and drinks. He drinks by throwing his head back and swallowing the contents in one go. He pours another

Pavel Will you have one?
Liszt No. (*He raises his hand*) It will give me a very thick head, and I have a very important day tomorrow. Besides, I still have my brandy.

Pavel drinks and again fills his glass. His mood is now slowly changing, his face becoming very grave

Are you all right, my friend? Is anything the matter?
Pavel Yes, yes I am all right.

Erna enters. She carries two buckets of hot water and cloths. She moves to the upstage corner and places the buckets down. She herself then kneels down with her back to Pavel's table, and begins to wash the floor. She uses one bucket to wash and one to rinse

For a moment Pavel watches her, then he drinks again, and again fills his glass. Liszt watches him waiting. For the first time, Pavel rises, adjusts his false arm, and moves to the fireplace. He stares down into it

Does the name Ekaterinburg mean anything to you?
Liszt Ekaterinburg . . . (*He thinks*) Why yes. That's the name of the town where the Tsar and all his family were murdered—or executed.
Pavel (*turning to Liszt*) You do well to draw a distinction.
Liszt Well, of course, it all depends on your political views.

Pavel Of course.

Liszt You were at Ekaterinburg?

Pavel Eventually. (*He moves back to the table and picks up his drink*) It was July nineteen eighteen. We had been at war with you for four long years and I too had lost many good friends, but somehow I had survived. (*He drinks*) The year before that, nineteen seventeen, the war had turned sour, at home the people were starving and there were bitter strikes. In March, the ultimate happened. Revolution. At the front the soldiers continued to fight. But all the time there were constant rumours, the Tsar had abdicated, the Tsar was dead. The Bolsheviks were in power. No-one was certain any more. For us, there seemed to be only two choices. The "Reds" or the "Whites"!

Liszt And which did you choose?

Pavel (*after a pause*) In my case the choice was made for me. (*He sits*) One morning after a particularly bloody offensive, my whole regiment was ordered back from the front. We were paraded in full kit, and addressed by our commanding officer. He told us in no uncertain terms just what the position was at home, and he made it quite clear, that the flag that was to fly at our head would be a "Red" one, and furthermore, because we were seasoned troops. We were to return immediately to Petrograd, to restore law and order in the streets.

Liszt So you became a Bolshevik? A Red Guard?

Pavel Yes, that was the name by which the world came to know us.

Liszt What happened to you then?

Pavel Our return to Petrograd never materialized. Events began to move very quickly. The Tsar abdicated, and nominated his brother, the Grand Duke Michael, to take his place. He declined to rule, and Russia, my Russia, became a Republic.

Liszt So you remained where you were?

Pavel No, instead we were moved to defend a garrison town on the eastern front.

Liszt And the name of the town?

Pavel Ekaterinburg.

There is a slight pause. Pavel and Liszt take their drinks. Erna rises and stacks two chairs on top of a table, then she returns quietly to her washing of the floor

Liszt (*curiously*) What month was this?

Pavel June.

Liszt Were the Tsar and his family already there when you arrived?

Pavel I don't know, perhaps! The first suspicion I had, was when rumours began to filter back, from soldiers who had been detailed for guard duty at the actual house where the Royal Family were being held.

Liszt Yes, I remember seeing photographs of the house. They were in all the newspapers.

Pavel There were stories of seeing faces at windows, and of the Tsar and his daughters walking together in the house grounds.

Liszt And is that how you came to see him again?

Pavel No. My last meeting with the Tsar came later, under different circumstances.

Liszt I see. Tell me. There is something not quite clear in my mind.

Pavel I know—you want me to tell you what my feelings were. Just exactly how my loyalties lay.

Liszt slowly nods his head

Can you understand me when I tell you that at that particular point in time, I did not know. I was not absolutely sure ... Perhaps that explains why, when the moment came for me to help him, I failed him.

Liszt Failed him, how? I don't understand. (*He leans forward intensely*)

Pavel drinks

Pavel It was a Monday evening. I had just finished mess when I was ordered to report to the officer of the day. I immediately went to his office, only to find on my arrival, another soldier already waiting. I knew his face, but not his name. We stood together, each of us frantically trying to remember just what exactly it was that we had done wrong. The door opened. "Enter". We marched in and came smartly to attention, caps in hand. "Because of your exemplary record in battle, you two men have been chosen for an important task. Report to the transport building at five o'clock tomorrow morning. I suggest you retire early! That is all!" We saluted and marched out. As you can imagine all that night I lay awake, trying to visualize what the task may be. At five the next morning, we were there, it was the same officer. He inspected our rifles, then handed me a piece of paper. "You will drive to this address and contact the man whose name is written here. On arrival you will take orders only from him." Without looking at the paper, I knew where the address would be.

Liszt It was that house.

Pavel Yes, the road from the camp to the town was about five miles, on each side, all the way, there was dense forest. When we arrived at the gates of the house, a guard stepped forward. I showed him the paper. He nodded. The gates opened. I drove in. Jacob Yurovsky, the man we were to contact, was waiting for us.

Liszt Was he a soldier?

Pavel No, at least I don't think so, he was wearing civilian clothes and he needed a shave. He read the paper and then he said "Follow me." We turned down a corridor and entered a room. (*He pauses, then drinks*)

Liszt Well?

Pavel rises and faces slightly front

Pavel It was a room about twenty foot by twelve foot. There were no windows. On the floor about a dozen mattresses, serving as makeshift beds, on the mattresses people were sleeping. They were covered by blankets and army greatcoats. In the corner an oil lamp on a small box giving off a dim yellow glow. On one side of it a man sat on a mattress his back against the wall. He was smoking a cigarette, and reading a book. At the other side, a woman wearing a dressing gown also sat propped against the wall. She was trying to do embroidery, but it was obvious that the light was not strong enough. I recognized them immediately. It was the Emperor and Empress. Yurovsky said, "Nicholas Romanov, you will get dressed, please." The Tsar looked quickly at the Empress. She reached across and touched him. Then he stubbed out his cigarette, and got out of bed. His clothes were arranged neatly on a chair. He began to dress. It was absolutely silent, except for the sound of him dressing, and the ticking of a clock somewhere in the room. I just looked at the wall in front of me, the outline of where a picture had once hung, was barely recognizable—in the dim light . . . Then I felt it! Somebody was watching me. I glanced down, and lying almost at my feet was a young girl. She was plainly terrified, and she had pulled the bedclothes up over her face, so that only her eyes were visible. It was those eyes that now met mine, round with fear. In a split second she looked away towards her father, then back at me. The same eyes as his, deep and warm. The moment was broken again by Yurovsky's voice. "You will need your top-coat." The Tsar picked it up then crossed to the Tsarina. He bent and kissed her forehead, and whispered something to her which I could not hear. I saw her lips move in reply. Then he stood and gazed around the sleeping family. As soon as he saw the girl lying awake, he moved to her. I had to step back to let him pass. He knelt down beside her. "Don't worry, it's only another interrogation. More boring questions. Be good to your mother, Anastasia." Then he kissed the tip of his finger and touched the end of her nose with it. He rose, walked up to Yurovsky and said in a loud voice, "Now I am at your disposal." We left the house and moved back to the car; as we got there, I stepped forward and opened the back door for him to get in. He looked at me for a moment. Then he said "Thank you," and climbed in. Yurovsky beckoned me away from the car. "You know the military exercise area between here and your camp?" I replied that I did. "Good, you will take him there." "What for?" I asked. "Never mind, just take him."

Liszt Why were you taking him?

Pavel (*raising his hand, indicating that Liszt should not interrupt him*) I turned the car around and began to drive back. Dawn was just breaking, and the birds had started to sing. Every time I looked into my mirror I could see his face, his eyes. The eyes are the windows of the soul, you know. As I carried on driving I began to feel a tension building up inside me. This is it, I thought. This is my chance! I could jam on the brake pedal, throw my companion off guard, seize his rifle, and if necessary kill him—(*he stands*)—or I could stop the car and try to reason with him. "Listen, Comrade, if you feel as I, if you are with me, then we can help him. Save him! What do you say?" There was sweat on my forehead, and my hands were sticking to the wheel. I glanced into the mirror. His face, his eyes; then at my companion. Do it, do it now! (*Pause*) I stopped the car. We were there. It was a large clearing in the forest. There were men waiting. Now it was too late. There was a group of ten Red Guards just standing and talking, casually holding their rifles. Three other men, one of whom I later found out was the Chairman of the Soviet, walked up to the car. He, the Chairman, opened the rear door, and said, "Get out, please." The Tsar did as he was asked. The Chairman then took the Tsar's arm and walked him into the centre of the clearing, about ten yards in front of the group of Red Guards. The Guards were now forming a straight line facing the Tsar. The Chairman read out the sentence of death. The Tsar lifted his head slightly, and said, "I would like to say good-bye to my wife, and children." "Your request is refused." The Chairman turned around and walked back towards us. The Guards raised their rifles and then . . . The birds stopped singing—as if the whole world had come to a halt. Then it was over!

Liszt My God!

Pavel (*quietly*) Well, do you believe me?

Liszt Yes. (*He shakes his head*) I don't know.

Pavel It's perfectly simple, either you do or you don't. (*He sits*)

Liszt (*taking a drink*) What you have told me is possible—but— I don't know. Everyone believes that the Tsar and the complete Royal Family, were killed at that house in Ekaterinburg—or at least that is what we were told.

Pavel Exactly! That is what you were told.

Liszt Yes. But don't you see? If your story is true, then the other one is false, or part of it at any rate.

Pavel I have no reason to doubt that the rest of the Royal Family were murdered, and in precisely the way that the reports issued by the powers in charge at that time described.

Liszt But it presents too great a conflict of stories. In the official details, there is no mention, no mention whatsoever, of the fact that the Tsar and his family were not all together at the time of their deaths. They were there, in the very same room! *All* of them.

Pavel So you don't believe me.

Liszt (*thinking hard*) No! And I'll tell you why. You are a journalist, or so you say. If your story is true, then, my God, why don't you publish it. With your professional contacts, surely you could find witnesses. One of those Red Guards, the firing squad! One of them must still be alive. Then there's the money. You could make a fortune. So why don't you, eh?

Pavel (*quietly*) It would be my thirty pieces of silver.

Liszt (*staring hard at Pavel*) You make it hard for me to know the truth, my friend.

Pavel (*raising his glass*) Then to hell with the truth. As the history of the world proves, the truth has no bearing on anything.

Liszt looks at Pavel, slightly startled, then winks an eye

Liszt Ah'ah. My friend, you have been pulling my leg—yes!

Pavel Perhaps! (*He drinks*)

Liszt Yes, you have. I can tell now! Why you devil, and you told it so convincingly. Still you are a journalist. (*He leans forward, not quite certain*) You are, aren't you?

Pavel Yes.

Liszt I knew it! Another thing which occurred to me, which would disprove your tale, is the woman's story.

Pavel What woman?

Liszt You remember, that woman who threw herself into the canal, off that bridge. Here! In Berlin. It was about ten years ago. Oh! You must remember! She claimed to be the only survivor, the Grand Duchess Anastasia. The young girl you saw, remember?

Pavel Yes, I remember. The girl with the frightened eyes.

Liszt Yes, that's the one. Now there *is* a fascinating story. Don't you think so? Anyway, she claims that she escaped the bullets because she fainted, and was covered by the others. But even she said that her father was there, with the rest of them.

Pavel She could be an impostor.

Liszt She could, but it is unlikely. Her story has been investigated and it would appear that a great many people are prepared to believe in her.

Pavel That's why I think she is an impostor. Any one member of that family who survived, after an ordeal like that, why, they would never want to be recognized, ever. There may be many prepared to believe her, but there are also many who would go to any lengths to see her dead. If she could really prove, without any doubt, who she really was.

Liszt Yes. That's a very good point. But if there had been a survivor . . . Let us say, for argument's sake, that it was the Grand Duchess Anastasia, surely it would be the ultimate in your career as a journalist, if you were to accidently come across her.

Pavel Someone who has lived all these years in secret, and wished it to remain so, would not be so easy to find.

Liszt She would have had to change herself completely. Become another person. Earn her living. Make friends. Get married even.

Pavel No. Marriage is too dangerous. If you want to remain undiscovered. She would need to produce a Birth Certificate; that could be very difficult. I think she would adopt a disguise that is so ordinary, so every day, that no one would ever question it.

Liszt What action would you take if you did find her.

Pavel I'd help her in every possible way I could.

Liszt You would not expose her?

Pavel No.

Liszt It certainly makes you think though. A disguise so ordinary, so every day, that no one would ever question it. Hmm . . . (*He thinks*)

Pavel takes a drink. Erna stands and places more chairs on to a table. The last one slips and falls to the floor. Liszt looks at her then leans across and whispers to Pavel

My friend, that's it. (*He points secretly to Erna*) Under our very noses all the time. It's perfect.

Pavel Don't be ridiculous. (*He pours another drink*).

Liszt But why not? She's the right age!

Pavel looks at Erna, then shakes his head

Pavel It's too obvious.

Liszt I don't understand, you just said . . .

Pavel Listen, in ten years time, when you try to recall this meeting, what is it you will remember most about me?

Liszt Well—I . . .

Pavel This! (*He moves his false arm so that it is clearly visible*) This is what you will remember. Right!

Liszt nods

See what I mean. That's why she is too obvious. (*He adjusts his arm to a more natural position*)

Liszt (*shrugging*) Just a thought. But it could have been. Let's see what she really looks like. (*He lightly throws his fork across the floor so that it lands in front of Erna*)

Erna stops working, picks the fork up, then looks across at Liszt

Come here, please. (*He gestures*) Come!

Erna rises and moves to Liszt

Erna Awr no . . . (*She points to Liszt's supper plate and then to her mouth*)

Liszt No, no more thank you. (*To Pavel*) Well, what do you think, if we washed her face, and gave her an expensive dress? (*Pavel makes no response*) Let me see your hands. (*He signals to Erna for her to show her hands*) Oh! Well we would have to do something with those. Let's see your feet!

Erna Gur-da. (*She is now completely lost, and has no idea what Liszt is trying to get her to do*)

Liszt Your feet. (*He points to his foot, then to Erna's*) Feet!

Erna very hesitantly lifts one foot

Oh yes, very dainty. Can you dance?

Erna, again not understanding, shakes her head

You know—dance? (*He stamps his feet and claps his hands*) Like this.

Erna now understands. She smiles broadly and nods her head in time to the clapping hands

Come on, then. Let's see you!

Erna lifts her skirt slightly and begins a girlish type of dance step, almost on the spot. The dance is by no means undignified or foolish

That's good. Very good! (*He continues to stamp and clap*)

Frau Ghirstfeld enters from the inner door. She carries an oil lamp

Frau Ghirstfeld Erna, what are you doing? (*She goes to Erna and scolds her gently*) Erna, the floor! (*She points*) Have you finished the floor? (*To the others*) I'm sorry, gentlemen. Was she troubling you?

Erna returns to her washing

Liszt (*rather sheepishly*) Oh! No! I'm afraid it was my fault. You see . . .

Frau Ghirstfeld Well, no matter. I've brought another lamp. (*She places it on the mantlepiece*) Oh, and she's let the fire go. (*She pokes the fire and puts on a couple of logs*) As if I haven't enough to do. Is there anything else I can get you two gentlemen?

Liszt No, I don't think so.

Pavel shakes his head

Frau Ghirstfeld Erna. (*She moves back to Erna*) Where are you up to? (*Gently*) When I said go quietly, I didn't mean go slowly as well. (*She inspects the floor*) I don't know how you can manage in this light? See, look here by the door, you'll have to do this again! And just look at your water, it's filthy. You'll have to get some fresh. Come I'll light the boiler for you.

(*She signals for Erna to follow*)

Erna picks up her rinsing bucket

Erna and Frau Ghirstfeld exit by the inner door

Liszt Damn and blast.
Pavel What's the matter?
Liszt Well, I feel such a heel!
Pavel Oh, you mean that just now.
Liszt Yes.
Pavel I wouldn't feel too badly about it. Probably the first bit of fun she's had all day. (*He drinks*)
Liszt Yes.

The Woman enters from the inner door. She now wears her top-coat and carries her handbag. She moves down to the fireplace, takes out her compact and begins to make up her face

As a point of interest, that is, if you don't mind talking about it, how did you come to lose your arm?
Pavel A tunnelling project I was involved in. Three years ago. There was a roof caved in. I was trapped. Unfortunately this was the only way I could be got out.
Liszt I see.

Woman (*moving across between the two men and placing her arm around Liszt's neck*) Is one of you two kind gentlemen going to offer me a drink?

Liszt (*removing her arm from his shoulder*) Not now. You've chosen the wrong time.

Pavel On the contrary. I think it's exactly the right time. I think you might be just what I need. (*From this point onwards he sinks by degrees into alcoholic oblivion*) Won't you join us?

Woman Thank you. (*She takes a chair from the table above the fireplace and sits between the two men, but closer to Pavel*) Perhaps it's you who should offer me a drink.

Pavel Vodka!

Woman (*shrugging lazily*) Anything!

Pavel pours her a drink

Are you staying the night?

Pavel nods

I'm available.

Liszt What about your other client, won't he miss you?

Woman Him, huh . . . (*She shrugs again*) He passed out on me. (*She drinks*) I must have been too much for him. Anyway, he was only a boy. I prefer a man. (*She looks suggestively at Pavel*) It's more interesting. (*She laughs in a loud, vulgar way*)

Liszt I should not have thought it mattered, as long as they can pay.

Woman It doesn't. (*She looks at him, brazenly*)

Liszt Are you expensive?

Woman You only get what you pay for. (*She picks up Pavel's book*) Whose is this? (*She flips the pages*)

Pavel Mine.

Woman It seems very complicated.

Pavel Not really.

Liszt My friend is a qualified engineer.

Woman Is that so. (*She stops at a particular page. She reads for a moment*) What's an Archimedes Screw? (*She looks cheekily at Pavel*)

Pavel It's a pump, used for lifting a liquid from one level to another.

Woman Oh, is that right? And I suppose every good gentleman should have one, eh! (*She laughs again in the same vulgar way*)

Liszt and Pavel do not respond

Oh, I'm sorry. Have I offended you? (*She makes a natural gesture and holds the book up to her face. Only her eyes are now visible*)

Pavel stares at her

What's the matter?
Pavel What? (*He continues to stare*)
Woman Why are you staring at me?
Pavel Was I?
Woman Yes. (*She moves closer to him*) Do you find me attractive?
Liszt If you'll excuse me, I must make a call, and I better find out where my room is. I won't be a moment.

Liszt rises and exits by the inner door

Woman You didn't answer my question. Do you like me?

She tries to start the glass game, but Pavel wants to talk

Pavel Are you German?
Woman (*with a lazy shrug*) What else. (*She points at Pavel*) You're not!
Pavel No, I'm Russian.
Woman Oh, I hear that Russian men are very wild lovers, is that right?
Pavel Possible. Would you like to see a photograph of my home? (*He takes out his wallet and opens it on the table*)

Woman If you like. (*She stares down at the wallet. It is quite fat and could hold a lot of money*)
Pavel Here you are.
Woman (*taking the photo*) Oh! It's very nice. Were you born there.
Pavel Yes, that was my room when I was a boy.

Erna enters with a fresh bucket of hot water. She goes to the outer door, kneels down, and begins again to wash the area around it

Woman When did you leave home?
Pavel When I was fifteen. (*He fills both glasses, takes his own, rises and moves to the fireplace. He stands looking down into it*)

I wanted to be an engineer. That meant college and hopefully university. But to enable me to study I had to have money.

The Woman gives a quick look to see if Erna is watching, but Erna's back is towards her. She slowly reaches out for the wallet, she starts to remove the money

And that would only be possible if I could find a job somewhere. (*He turns quickly and catches the woman with the money in her hand*)

Just as I thought. Give that back to me, please. (*He holds his hand out*)

Woman (*viciously*) Well, what did you expect! (*She tosses the wallet back to him*)

Pavel (*standing over her*) Let me see your permit?

Woman Permit!

Pavel Yes. You do have one, don't you?

Woman Of course I have.

Pavel Then show it to me.

Woman It's—it's in my other bag.

Pavel You're lying. (*He sits*)

Woman I'm not.

Pavel (*after a pause*) I am going to report you to the police. (*Pause*) You're not German are you.

Woman (*changing completely, her harshness gone*) No, please, don't do that. Look, I'll tell you the truth. You're right. I haven't got a permit.

Pavel Why not?

She hesitates

Why not?

Woman Because—well, you see ... (*Becoming very frightened*) You're right, I was not born in Germany, I entered the country illegally. (*She looks to see if Erna is watching, but she is still scrubbing*) And if you report me to the police, then—then they will start to question me, and—well, you see, the truth is —oh God!

Pavel (*unable to stand her agony any longer*) Stop! I don't want to hear any more.

Woman What do you mean?

Pavel Here take this. (*He gives her the money*)
Woman I don't understand.
Pavel Just take it, and go!

She hesitates

   Go!
Woman Will you report me? Will you?
Pavel (*quietly*) No, I won't report you.
Woman Thank you. (*She rises and moves to the inner door*)

   Herr Liszt enters. The Woman stops, looks back at Pavel, then walks quickly out

Liszt What's happened there? You looked all set for the night when I went out.
Pavel I changed my mind.
Liszt Rather attractive I thought, in a common sort of way of course.
Pavel Of course. (*He takes a drink from the bottle*) Do you believe that life gives you a second chance?
Liszt Sorry, I don't follow. (*He sits*)
Pavel A second chance to help to make something right, that you did wrong a long time ago.
Liszt I'm still not with you.
Pavel (*with a little laugh*) No, why should you be. (*He drinks again from the bottle*)
Liszt Well it's almost one. (*He looks at his watch*) I'm off to my bed, what about you?
Pavel No, not yet.
Liszt You should you know. You look all in.
Pavel I'll be all right.
Liszt It's good night, then. What about that lift in the morning. Will you take it?
Pavel (*thinking*) Yes, yes, I will.
Liszt (*rising*) Good, I'll see you at breakfast. It's been a most enjoyable meeting. You know, you almost had me going for a time. (*He wags his finger at Pavel*) But I forgive you.

   Liszt picks up his case and exits by the inner door

Pavel I forgive you—if only it were as simple as that—that's all I want—to be forgiven. (*He rises and moves unsteadily to the* *fireplace*) It was his eyes, you see. Did I tell you that the eyes are the windows of the soul? (*He stares into the lamp*) They illuminate everything, like a bright flame, deep and warm. (*Suddenly he turns and stares at Erna. Then he positions his false arm at a right angle, his hand above his head. He quickly hangs the lamp handle on to the fingers of the hand and moves, staggering slightly, to Erna. He lifts her by her elbow, turns her, and draws her to him. He stares down into her face*)

The lamp hangs between them. It illuminates their faces. Erna stares back. She is petrified

What do you see in my eyes? (*He shakes her*) Tell me. What? Is it guilt? Pain?

She makes an unintelligible sound and tries to pull away

Do you believe that the eyes are the window of the soul? Do you?

Again she makes a sound and shakes her head

Tell me! (*He shakes her, and this time he shouts loudly*) Tell me!

Erna continues to look up at him, and makes a series of quiet, unintelligible sounds. He relaxes his grip and turns away, swaying slightly

No, you can't tell me, can you.

Erna gently pulls at his arm. He turns back to her. She joins her hands together and lays the side of her face on them and closes her eyes, as if asleep. Then she points to Pavel, and to herself, then to the room above

(*Softly*) No, that's not what I want. You can't give me what I want. (*He moves back to his table and sits*)

Erna watches him for a moment, then kneels and resumes her washing, her back to him. Pavel places the lamp on the table and adjusts his arm. Then he picks up the bottle and tries to drink. The bottle is empty

(*His voice very hushed*) It was my fault, you see. Mine. I could have saved him. There was a—chance. My children—I give you my blessing—I give you . . . Now I am at your disposal.

The birds stopped singing—singing . . . Oh my Tsar—forg-i-v-e
m-e . . . (*He sleeps. The bottle rolls from his hand*)

*Erna stops washing and sits back on her heels. She pauses. Then
she turns and looks at Pavel. She rises to her feet and walks,
slowly and with dignity, to his table. She touches him on his temple.
He does not stir*

Erna May God bless you, Pavel Alexandrovich. When I pray to
my father I will ask him to forgive you.

*Erna gently strokes his hair, then turns, walks back to her place,
kneels down, and goes on with her work as—*

the CURTAIN *slowly falls*

FURNITURE AND PROPERTY LIST

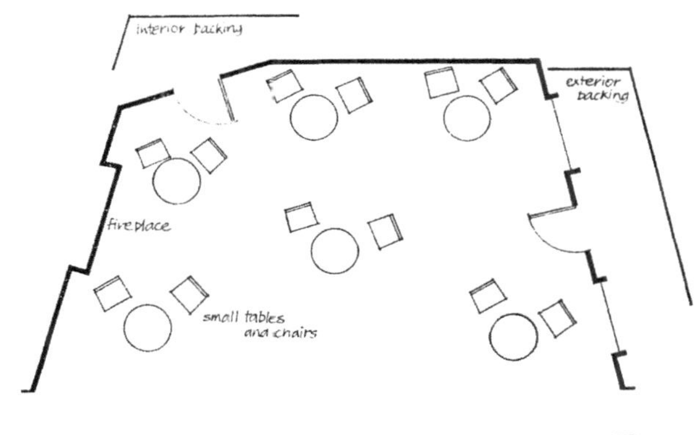

On stage: 6 small tables. *On* **Pavel's** *table:* lamp, book, bottle of Schnapps, glass. *On* **Man's** *table:* bottle of Schnapps, glass, lamp
12 small chairs
Broom (for **Erna**)
On floor: sawdust
On outer door: bolt
In fireplace: basket of logs
Window curtains

Off stage: Flour **(Frau Ghirstfeld)**
Small case **(Liszt)**
Tray with half-bottle of brandy, glass **(Erna)**
Tray with bowl of broth, plate of brown bread, plate of cold German sausage, knife, fork, spoon **(Erna)**
Bucket, shovel **(Frau Ghirstfeld)**
Tray with bottle of vodka, glass **(Frau Ghirstfeld)**
2 buckets of hot water, cloths **(Erna)**
Oil lamp **(Frau Ghirstfeld)**

Personal: **Woman:** handbag with powder compact
Pavel: wallet with photograph and notes
Liszt: wristwatch

LIGHTING PLOT

Property fittings required: pendant, wall brackets (dressing only), 4 oil or paraffin lamps, log fire effect

An inn room

To open: Night. All oil lamps and fire lit

No cues